NATURE DETECTIVE

British Mammals

Victoria Munson

Published in paperback in 2014 by Wayland
Copyright © Wayland 2014

Wayland
338 Euston Road
London NW1 3BH

Wayland Australia
Level 17/207 Kent Street
Sydney, NSW 2000

Designer: Elaine Wilkinson

Picture acknowledgements:
Shutterstock: cpphotoimages 3(tl);
scattoselvaggio 3(tr); Marek Velechovsky
4(tr); CreativeNature.nl 4(bl); Steven Ward
5(tl); Elaine Nash 6; Richard Bowden 7;
Kichigin 8; D. Kucharski/ K. Kucharska 9;
Ian Rentoul 10; Sandy Hedgepeth 11; S.
Cooper Digital 12; Ian Rentoul 13; Oligo
14; Matthijs Wetterauw 15; Scattoselvaggio
16; CreativeNature.nl 17; CreativeNature.
nl 18; CreativeNature.nl 20; CreativeNature.
nl 21; Andy Poole 22; Martin Fowler
23; CreativeNature.nl 24; IrinaK 25;
CreativeNature.nl 26; CreativeNature.nl 29;
Stephen Farhall 30; Gucio_55 31; BMJ 32;
belizar 33; Ivan Kuzmin 35; cpphotoimages
39; Christopher Mills 40; Steven Ward 41;
Elaine Nash 43; Richard Bowden 44; Rick
Wylie 45; chris2766 47; Marek Velechovsky
48; Beth Schroeder 51; George Hachey 53;
Gillian Holliday 54; Swellphotography 55;

Ian Rentoul 56(t); Sandy Hedgepeth (56(b);
Ian Rentoul 58; Kichigin 59; Martin Fowler
62; Ivan Kuzmin 63; Swellphotography 64;
Corbis: Ocean/Corbis 1; Stephen Dalton/
Minden Pictures/Corbis 2(bl); Richard
Herrmann/Minden Pictures/Corbis 2(br);
Ocean/Corbis 3(bl); Solvin Zankl/Visuals
Unlimited/Corbis 3(br); Dietmar Nill/ Foto
Natura/Minden Pictures/Corbis 4(br); John
Short/Design Pics/Design Pics/Corbis 5(tl);
Stephen Dalton/Minden Pictures/Corbis 19;
Lothar Lenz/Corbis 27; Derek Middleton/
FLPA/Minden Pictures/Corbis 28; Dietmar
Nill/ Foto Natura/Minden Pictures/Corbis 34;
DK Limited/CORBIS 36; Dietmar Nill/ Foto
Natura/Minden Pictures/Corbis 37; Stephen
Dalton/Minden Pictures/Corbis 38; John
Short/Design Pics/Design Pics/Corbis 42;
Ocean/Corbis 46; Steve Austin; Papilio/
CORBIS 49; Richard Herrmann/Minden
Pictures/Corbis 50; Solvin Zankl/Visuals
Unlimited/Corbis 52; Swellphotography 64.
Artwork page 56, 57, 58, 59: Peter Bull.

A cataloguing record for this title is available
at the British Library.
Dewey number: 599.0941

ISBN: 978 0 7502 8342 7

Printed in China

10 9 8 7 6 5 4 3 2

Wayland is a division of Hachette Children's
Books, an Hachette UK company.
www.hachette.co.uk

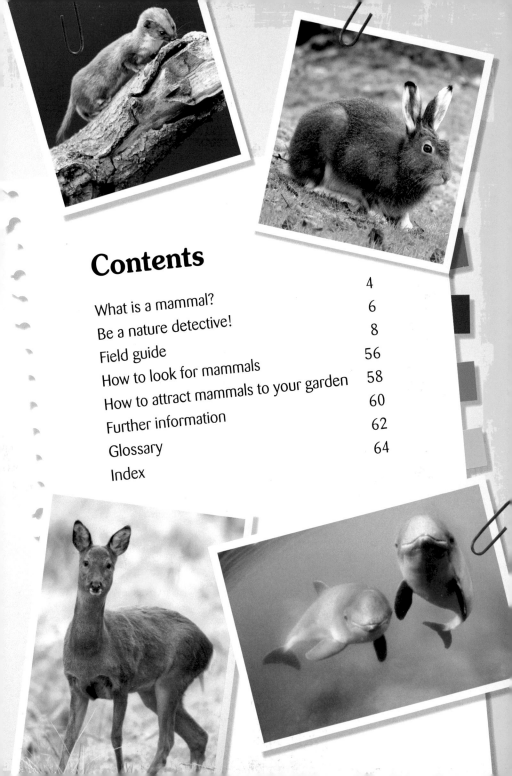

Contents

What is a mammal?

A mammal is an animal that breathes air, has a backbone and can produce milk to feed its young. All mammals have hair at some stage in their life. For example, baby whales and dolphins are born with a moustache! Most mammals also have teeth. Mammals have only two sets of teeth - a baby set and an adult set. Reptiles and fish can get new teeth throughout their life.

Moving around

Mammals have different ways of getting around. Some mammals walk, such as deer and hedgehogs. Dolphins, seals and whales swim using flippers. Bats can fly.

Some mammals are active in the daytime (diurnal) like cows and horses; some are only active at night (nocturnal) such as bats and badgers. Others, such as house mice, are active day and night.

Muntjac Deer

Natterer's Bat

Bank Vole

Pine Marten

Otter

Mammal habitats

Mammals live all over the world in many different habitats. In tropical regions, there are mammals like tigers and elephants. Polar bears live near the North Pole. Camels and fennec foxes live in deserts. British mammals live in a variety of different habitats, from woodlands and parks to mountains, rivers and seas.

Endangered mammals

Some mammals in Britain are becoming rare due to habitat loss or pollution. Greater Horseshoe Bats roost in mines but when mining declined greatly, mines were closed up and the bats had nowhere to go. Introduced species such as the American Mink were eating so many Water Voles that they became endangered. Measures have been taken to protect both species and now their numbers are increasing again. However, there are always new threats and conservationists have to work hard to protect some species from extinction.

There are over 4,000 species of mammal in the world.

Be a nature detective!

To be a nature detective, you need to be observant, patient and quiet. Mammals scare easily and can be shy so it might take time before you can spot one. Listen carefully. Sometimes you can hear mammals before you see them.

Where to see mammals

You can see some mammals in your garden. Or you could take a nature walk through woodland, along a river or by the sea. There are different types of mammal in each habitat. You could ask to visit a different habitat at the weekend or for a school trip.

Scottish Wildcat

What to take

If you're going out to find mammals, you may need to wear wellies and a waterproof jacket. Take binoculars and a notebook and pens.

Waterproof jacket

Wellies

Pens

Magnifying glass

Binoculars

bushy tail

short ears

Eating nut

Making notes

Once you've spotted a mammal, use a notebook to help you record some details about it. Note down its colour, shape, size, where it was or what it was eating. This will help you to identify it later if you aren't sure what it is.

Be respectful of nature

When you're out and about looking at wildlife, always follow the countryside code.

Red Deer

The Countryside Code

1 Be safe – plan ahead and follow signs
2 Leave gates and property as you find them
3 Protect plants and animals, and take your litter home
4 Keep dogs under close control
5 Consider other people

Rabbit

Size: 35–40 cm
Latin name: *Oryctolagus cuniculus*
Habitat: Farmland, woodland, sand dunes and hillsides
Food: Grass and plants
Lifespan: Up to 10 years

A male rabbit is called a "buck", and a female rabbit is called a "doe".

White tail

Rabbits live in groups called colonies in burrows underground. They can mainly be seen at dawn and at dusk when they come out of their burrows to feed. Their main food is grass, but they will eat leaves, buds, tree bark and roots, too. They are easily startled and will thump the ground with their hind legs when alarmed.

When running from a predator, a hare can run as fast as 60 kph.

Long ears

Brown Hare

Size: 60–70 cm
Latin name: *Lepus europaeus*
Habitat: Farmland, woodland and fields
Food: Grass, plants and crops
Lifespan: 3–4 years

Hares have longer ears and legs than a Rabbit and are much bigger, but you are more likely to see a Hare than a Rabbit. Hares live above ground in open fields. In the daytime, they will hide in a scrape in the ground where they are partly hidden from sight. The best time to see them is at dawn and dusk when they are moving around looking for food.

Mountain Hare

Size: 60–70 cm
Latin name: *Lepus timidus*
Habitat: Farmland, woodland and fields
Food: Grass, plants and crops
Lifespan: 4 years

Mountain hares are native to
Britain and are now found mostly
in Scotland and the north of England.
When there is snow on the ground, they change
colour from brown to white to keep them camouflaged
although their tail is white all year round. They are active
in the evening and at night finding food. In the daytime, they
rest in scrapes in the ground sheltered by rocks and heather.

The Common Shrew needs to eat every 2–3 hours.

Common Shrew

Size: 7.5 cm
Latin name: *Sorex araneus*
Habitat: Hedgerows, meadows, marshes and woodland
Food: Insects, slugs, snails and worms
Lifespan: 2 years

As its name suggests, the Common Shrew is fairly common. It has a long, narrow nose, silky brown fur and a grey underside. It is always on the move, looking for food. Listen out and sometimes you might hear its high-pitched squeaks.

Pygmy Shrew

Size: 6 cm
Latin name: *Sorex minutus*
Habitat: Moors, woodland and farmland
Food: Insects, spiders, snails and slugs
Lifespan: 1–2 years

Pygmy shrews prefer to live on their own.

The Pygmy Shrew is Britain's smallest mammal. They have brown fur, a pointed nose and a round head. They look very similar to Common Shrews but they have a longer, thicker tail. They like to live alone. They are active day and night looking for food, because if they don't eat for more than two hours they will die.

A Pygmy Shrew weighs less than a 10 pence coin.

Water Shrew

Size: 10 cm
Latin name: *Neomys fodiens*
Habitat: Riverbanks and ponds
Food: Small fish, worms and water insects
Lifespan: Up to 18 months

Water shrews have venomous saliva that stuns their prey.

Water Shrews are the largest of the shrews. They have dark upperparts and white underparts. As their name suggests, these shrews are often seen near water. When you see them in the water, their fur will look silvery. They live in long burrows in riverbanks. While they can live for up to 18 months, most don't survive that long because they have many predators, such as birds of prey, pike and mink.

Hedgehog

Size: 16–25 cm
Latin name: *Erinaceus europaeus*
Habitat: Hedgerows, parks and gardens
Food: Beetles, worms and slugs
Lifespan: Up to 5 years

Don't feed hedgehogs milk and bread. This will make them ill. Try unsalted peanuts or grated cheese.

Hedgehogs have light-brown tipped spikes on their round bodies. An adult hedgehog will have between 5–7,000 spines. They are mostly nocturnal, meaning that you will usually only see them at night. In about October, when the weather starts to turn colder, hedgehogs hibernate. They dig a small hole and cover themselves with leaves, either under hedges, in gardens or in woodland. They come out when the weather gets a bit warmer again around April.

Mole

Size: 11–16 cm
Latin name: *Talpa europaea*
Habitat: Farms and woodland
Food: Grubs, worms and insects
Lifespan: 2–5 years

Male moles are called 'boars' and female moles are called 'sows'. A group of moles is called a 'labour'.

Moles have black, velvety fur and very strong, curved front paws for digging tunnels. They have small eyes and bad eyesight. Moles live in burrows underground. The molehills that you can see are waste soil from the tunnels they have dug. Mole tunnels may be up to 70 metres long. If moles don't eat every few hours, they will die.

Bank Vole

Size: 10 cm
Latin name: *Myodes glareolus*
Habitat: Deciduous woods and hedgerows
Food: Leaves, buds, berries and insects
Lifespan: Up to 2 years

Bank Voles use a network of tunnels to avoid predators. Their predators are owls, foxes and weasels.

Long
whiskers

The Bank Vole has a reddish-brown coat. They have more prominent ears and a longer tail than the Field Vole. They are active during the day and night, but rest often under logs, among tree roots, tree holes or underground. When they are active, they move very fast and are good climbers and swimmers.

Field Vole

Size: 11 cm
Latin name: *Microtus agrestis*
Habitat: Woodland, fields and open land
Food: Grass, leaves and moss
Lifespan: Up to 2 years

Rounded ears

The Field Vole is the main source of food for barn owls. They are also eaten by weasels, stoats, foxes and birds of prey.

The Field Vole (also known as the Short-tailed Vole) has grey-brown upperparts and cream-grey underparts. Their tail is much shorter than the Bank Vole's. They are active in the day. They make tunnels in open ground and can be seen running along in them.

Water Vole

Size: 19 cm
Latin name: *Arvicola terrestris*
Habitat: Ponds, canals, streams and marshes
Food: Waterside plants and snails
Lifespan: 5 months

The Water Vole is also known as the Water Rat.

Short tail

The Water Vole is the largest of the voles in the UK. They have dark brown fur, a short tail and long claws that are used for burrowing in muddy riverbanks. The skin between their toes is slightly webbed to help them swim.

Rats like to live in large groups.

Dark grey
fur

Brown Rat

Size: 22–27 cm
Latin name: *Rattus norvegicus*
Habitat: Urban areas
Food: Scraps of food
Lifespan: Up to 18 months

Rats have coarse brown
or dark grey fur, with lighter
coloured underparts and a thick, scaly
tail. They live in colonies in tunnels near
houses and eat food they find lying around.
Rats often groom each other and sleep together.

19

Wood Mouse

Size: 8–11 cm
Latin name: *Apodemus sylvaticus*
Habitat: Woods, hedgerows and gardens
Food: Berries, buds, nuts, seeds and insects
Lifespan: 12–18 months

Wood mice are very common.
They have honey-brown fur on their
upperparts and silvery-grey fur on their
underparts, with large ears and eyes. They make
their homes in tunnels underground. They are good
climbers and move quickly. They are mainly nocturnal
and have good night vision and sense of smell.

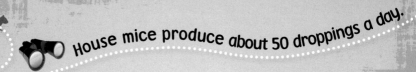

Large, round ears

House Mouse

Size: 8–10 cm
Latin name: *Mus musculus*
Habitat: Farmland and towns
Food: Cereals, seeds, vegetables and fruit
Lifespan: 1–2 years

The House Mouse's grey-brown fur and large ears makes it distinct from other mice. House mice live near humans and will eat crops and food. They are good climbers, jumpers and swimmers, using their tail for balance. They are mostly nocturnal.

Harvest Mouse

Size: 6–7 cm
Latin name: *Micromys minutus*
Habitat: Fields and farmland
Food: Soft leaves, insects and seeds
Lifespan: 12–18 months

The Harvest Mouse
is Britain's smallest rodent.
They have brown fur with either a
red or a yellow tinge, and white underparts.
Their tail is as long as their body and they use it to
climb up plant stems. Harvest Mice make tennis-ball-
sized nests of woven grasses in corn and grass stalks.

Dormouse

Size: 8 cm
Latin name: *Muscardinus avellanarius*
Habitat: Hedgerows and woodland, mostly hazel trees
Food: Flowers, nuts and fruits
Lifespan: 5 years

There are estimated to be only 80,000 Dormice left in Britain.

This mouse is rarely seen because it is nocturnal and hibernates for a large part of the year. They have golden-brown fur and large black eyes. From October to May, they hibernate in the crooks of trees or in log piles. If the weather is cold when they come out of hibernation, they will curl back up into a ball and go back to sleep.

23

Edible Dormouse

Size: 13–15 cm
Latin name: *Glis glis*
Habitat: Woodland, parks and orchards
Food: Nuts, fruit, insects and flowers
Lifespan: Up to 7 years

The Edible Dormouse
is the largest of the dormice.
They have a grey coat and a long
bushy tail. Introduced to Britain in 1902, there
are now thought to be about 10,000 Edible
Dormice, mostly found in the Chilterns. They are good
climbers and spend most of their time in trees.

Yellow-necked Field Mouse

Size: 10 cm
Latin name: *Apodemus flavicollis*
Habitat: Woodland, hedgerows and urban areas
Food: Cereals, seeds, vegetables and fruit
Lifespan: 1 year

The Yellow-necked Field Mouse looks like a Wood Mouse, but is larger and has a yellowish collar on its throat. They have sandy-brown fur and white underparts. They are very good at climbing trees, which helps them find food in high branches.

They can jump up to 90 cm high (nine times their own height!)

Grey Squirrel

Size: 27 cm
Latin name: *Sciurus carolinensis*
Habitat: Parks, gardens and woodland
Food: Seeds, acorns and nuts
Lifespan: 3–6 years

Large, bushy tail

Long claws

The Grey Squirrel was introduced to
Britain from North America in the nineteeth
century and is now Britain's most common squirrel.
They can be found throughout England south of Cumbria,
in Wales and in parts of Scotland. Squirrels are well known for
burying food to eat later. Some food stores are dug up again after a
few hours, while some are found a few months later. Grey Squirrels have
very good memories and use landmarks and smell to find their stores again.

A squirrel's nest, made of leaves and twigs, is called a 'drey'.

Large, tufted ears

Red Squirrel

Size: 20–28 cm
Latin name: *Sciurus vulgaris*
Habitat: Conifer woods
Food: Seeds of cones, berries, birds' eggs and nuts
Lifespan: 7 years

The Red Squirrel is Britain's native squirrel. However, it is now not that common apart from in the north of England, Anglesey, the Isle of Wight and in the Scottish Highlands. Red Squirrels have red fur, a white belly and distinct tufts coming off their ears. Its long bushy tail helps the squirrel to balance and steer when moving from tree to tree.

Common Pipistrelle Bat

Wingspan: 20–23 cm
Latin name: *Pipistrellus pipistrellus*
Habitat: Woodland, farmland and towns
Food: Insects
Lifespan: Up to 16 years

One Pipistrelle Bat will eat up to 3,000 insects in one night.

These are the most common British bats
and they are also the smallest. They have dark-brown
to rusty coloured fur on their back, and yellowish-brown
fur on their underside. Their nose and ears are black. At dusk,
they come out of their roost, in lofts and buildings, to find food. If you
see one flying, it will have a jerky flight pattern. From mid-November to
April, they hibernate in building crevices, bat boxes, trees and cellars.

Brown Long-eared Bat

Wingspan: 23–28 cm
Latin name: *Plecotus auritus*
Habitat: Gardens, woodland and farmland
Food: Insects
Lifespan: Up to 30 years

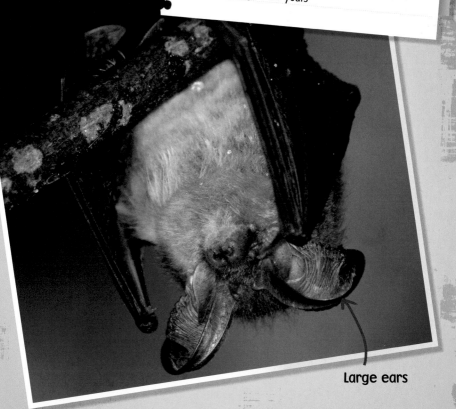

Large ears

As their name suggests, these bats have very long ears! Their ears help them to listen for insects. When resting, they curl them back or tuck them under their wings. They have brown-grey long fluffy fur. They sometimes fly in the day as well as at night, but are easy prey for predators, especially cats, because they fly slowly and close to the ground.

Daubenton's Bat

Wingspan: 24–27 cm
Latin name: *Myotis daubentonii*
Habitat: Woodland, towns and water
Food: Insects
Lifespan: Up to 22 years

These bats can often be seen
flying low over lakes and ponds at
sunset. Their large feet help them to pick up
prey from the water. They have grey or dark-brown fur
on upperparts and silvery-grey underparts. Their face is
pinkish-brown. From October until April, they hibernate.

Noctule Bat

Wingspan: 32–40 cm
Latin name: *Nyctalis noctula*
Habitat: Woodland, gardens and parks
Food: Insects
Lifespan: Up to 12 years

Noctule bats can fly at 50 km an hour!

One of the largest bats in Britain, this bat has reddish-brown fur and broad ears. They can be found flying in the day or at sunset. They have a distinctive high and fast flight with turns and dives. Noctule Bats mainly live in trees, although they will also roost in buildings and street lights. In winter, they hibernate in hollow trees, buildings and rock crevices.

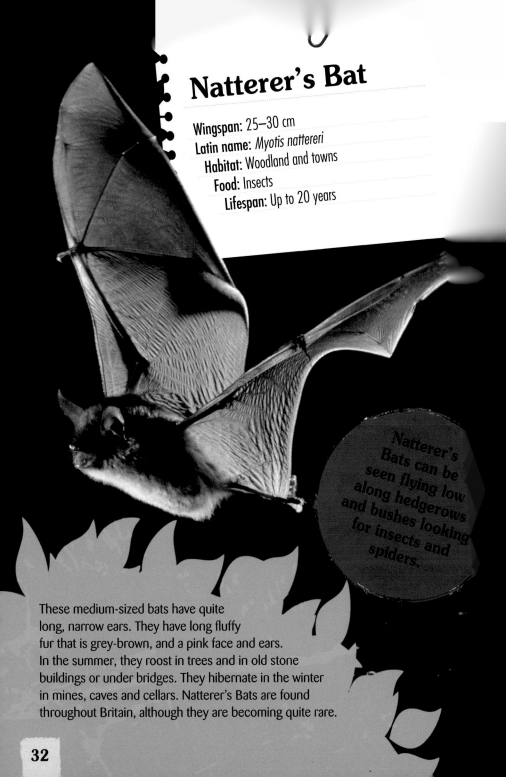

Natterer's Bat

Wingspan: 25–30 cm
Latin name: *Myotis nattereri*
Habitat: Woodland and towns
Food: Insects
Lifespan: Up to 20 years

Natterer's Bats can be seen flying low along hedgerows and bushes looking for insects and spiders.

These medium-sized bats have quite long, narrow ears. They have long fluffy fur that is grey-brown, and a pink face and ears. In the summer, they roost in trees and in old stone buildings or under bridges. They hibernate in the winter in mines, caves and cellars. Natterer's Bats are found throughout Britain, although they are becoming quite rare.

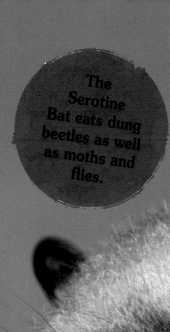

Serotine Bat

Wingspan: 32–38 cm
Latin name: *Eptesicus serotinus*
Habitat: Countryside, park and woodland
Food: Insects
Lifespan: Up to 19 years

This large bat has dark-brown fur on its upperparts and light-brown underparts. Their nose and triangular-shaped ears are black. They often fly high up. They are usually found in small groups in roosts in hollow trees, lofts and barns. The Serotine Bat is a less common species in Britain, and can be found only across the south and east of England and in South Wales.

Lesser Horseshoe Bat

Wingspan: 20–25 cm
Latin name: *Rhinolophus hipposideros*
Habitat: Woodland and open grassland areas.
Food: Insects
Lifespan: Up to 21 years

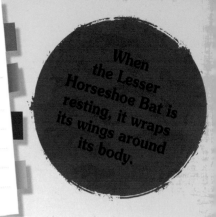

When the Lesser Horseshoe Bat is resting, it wraps its wings around its body.

The Lesser Horseshoe Bat is one of the smallest British bats, about the size of a plum. They have a horseshoe-shaped flap of skin as a nose. These bats roost in the day in caves and cellars and come out at night to search for moths. They can be found in south-west England and across Wales. In summer, they roost in attics, barns and stables. From September to May, they hibernate in caves, tunnels, mines and cellars.

Greater Horseshoe Bat

Wingspan: 35–40 cm
Latin name: *Rhinolophus ferrumequinum*
Habitat: Farmland and woodland
Food: Insects
Lifespan: Up to 30 years

The Greater Horseshoe Bat is one of the largest bats in Britain and is about the size of a small pear. They are recognisable by their sharply pointed, leaf-shaped ears. They have ash-grey upperparts, although an older adult may look reddish. They are completely nocturnal, only leaving their roost when it is dark. The Greater Horseshoe Bat gets its name from its horseshoe-shaped nose.

Badger

Size: 80–95 cm
Latin name: *Meles meles*
Habitat: Woodland
Food: Slugs, earthworms, roots, frogs, lizards and small mammals
Lifespan: Up to 14 years

A group of badgers is known as a 'clan'.

Badgers have a distinctive black and white stripy face. However, they are rarely seen because they only come out at night to feed. In the daytime, they live in an underground network of tunnels called 'setts'. With their curved claws, they can dig a deep tunnel in under two minutes. Each sett may have up to 20 entrances and be more than 100 metres long. Nest chambers are lined with dry grass, bracken and straw. Some badger setts are hundreds of years old. They keep them clean by taking their bedding up to tunnel entrances to air.

Large, pointed ears

Fox

Size: 1–1.2 m
Latin name: *Vulpes vulpes*
Habitat: Farmland, woodland and towns
Food: Mammals, birds and insects
Lifespan: 2–3 years in the wild

Foxes have pointed ears and the same body shape as a dog. They have reddy-orange fur with a bushy, white-tipped tail. Foxes are brilliant hunters, able to sprint and jump. They live in dens hollowed out under a tree root, or sometimes they will live in badger setts. Foxes bury any food they don't eat to come back to later.

Stoat

Size: 35–40 cm
Latin name: *Mustela erminea*
Habitat: Woodland, farmland and mountains
Food: Rabbits, small rodents, birds and eggs
Lifespan: Up to 3 years

A group of stoats is called a 'caravan'.

A stoat has a long slender body, orange-
brown upperparts and white underparts.
They have a long tail with a black tip. Northern
stoats, called ermine, are white in winter, but always have
a black tip on their tail. Stoats have a good sense of sight,
smell and hearing, which they use to help them hunt. If you listen
out for the squeals of a rabbit, you might see a stoat because rabbits
are their favourite food. Stoats are very good climbers and climb trees
to take baby birds from their nests. They are also strong swimmers.

Wide head

Weasel

Size: 20—25 cm
Latin name: *Mustela nivalis*
Habitat: Woodland, farmland and mountains
Food: Small mammals and birds
Lifespan: 2—3 years

Weasels look like stoats, but they are smaller and do not have a black tip on their tail. They also have similar habitats, but tend to stay out of each other's way. Weasels are nocturnal and come out at night to look for food. They run with an arched back, and their long slender bodies help them to follow prey into small burrows.

Short, brown fur

American Mink

- **Size:** 42–65 cm
- **Latin name:** *Neovison vison*
- **Habitat:** Near water
- **Food:** Water birds, fish and waterside small mammals
- **Lifespan:** 8 years

This chocolate-brown animal is often mistaken for an Otter because they look similar and both live near water. However, the American Mink is much smaller. American Minks escaped from fur farms in the 1950s and have since bred rapidly. Nowadays, steps are being taken to remove them from Scotland because they are reducing the numbers of other native British wildlife such as Water Voles and Moorhens.

Otter

Size: 95–130 cm
Latin name: *Lutra lutra*
Habitat: Rivers, lakes and coastal waters
Food: Fish, crabs, eels, frogs and sea urchins
Lifespan: 3–4 years

The Otter has brown fur with a long body, short legs and a thick tail. Otters are brilliant swimmers and they use their tail and webbed feet to push them through the water. They can stay underwater for a few minutes. Their ears and nostrils close automatically when they dive.

Pine Martens sometimes have blue poo in summer because they eat so many bilberries.

Pine Marten

Size: 65–75 cm
Latin name: *Martes martes*
Habitat: Mountain woods
Food: Squirrels, mammals and birds
Lifespan: Up to 10 years

Pine Martens are the size of a domestic cat, but with a longer, thinner body. They have a reddish-brown coat with a creamy-yellow throat and chest. They are mainly found in the Scottish Highlands, but sometimes in North Wales and the north of England, too. They like to live in dens in hollow trees, or in cliff and rock crevices, because they are very good climbers.

Scottish Wildcat

Size: 56 cm
Latin name: *Felis silvestris grampia*
Habitat: Scottish highlands
Food: Rabbits, small mammals, fish and frogs
Lifespan: 6–8 years

There are now thought to be only 40 Scottish Wildcats alive.

Although Scottish Wildcats look very similar to domestic cats, Wildcats are twice as big and can't be tamed. They look like tabby cats and have thick brown-and-black-striped fur. Their face is wider than a domestic cat's and their tail is thicker, with a black tip. They are active at dawn and dusk and hunt across a large territory up to 10 km wide. They mark their territory with their scent. They live alone, only meeting up in mid-winter to mate.

Red Deer

Size: 1.15–1.2 m
Latin name: *Cervus elaphus*
Habitat: Open countryside and woods
Food: Grass, fruit and tree bark
Lifespan: Up to 10 years

Broad antlers

The Red Deer is Britain's largest native land mammal. The male is much larger than the female, with branching antlers which he sheds each February. The antlers grow again in the spring, and each year they grow back a bit bigger. In summer, their coat is reddish-brown; in winter it is grey-brown. Red Deer are active from dusk till dawn.

Large, flat antlers

Fallow Deer

Size: 85–95 cm
Latin name: *Dama dama*
Habitat: Parks and woodland
Food: Herbs, grass, berries, acorns and leaves
Lifespan: 12–16 years

Male deer are called 'bucks' and females are called 'does'.

The Fallow Deer is smaller than the Red Deer, but larger than the Roe Deer. They have tan-coloured coats with white spots. The spots sometimes become less obvious in winter. They are often kept in parks and live in herds. The male has antlers that have broad flattened ends. Fallow deer are herbivores, which means they eat all types of vegetation, such as shoots and leaves, berries and grass.

Roe Deer

Size: 65–70 cm
Latin name: *Capreolus capreolus*
Habitat: Woodland
Food: Leaves, herbs and berries
Lifespan: 5–10 years

The Roe Deer is smaller
than the Red Deer and Fallow Deer.
They have a grey-brown to black coat in
winter and a reddish-brown coat in summer with
a whitish patch on their rump. The male has small,
ridged branched antlers that are shed in November.

Sika Deer

Size: 80–95 cm
Latin name: Cervus nippon
Habitat: Woodland
Food: Leaves, herbs and berries
Lifespan: Up to 15 years

Sika deer were a present to King Edward VII in the 1900s, but they escaped and bred.

In winter, Sika Deer have grey-brown coats; in summer they are reddish-brown with white spots. They are a similar size to Fallow Deer, but have a darker colouring. The male has narrow antlers with few branches, which are shed in April. Sikas live alone for most of the year, but come together in small groups in the winter. They are mostly found in the New Forest, in Hampshire.

Muntjac Deer

Size: 45–48 cm
Latin name: *Muntiacus reevesi*
Habitat: Woodland and farmland
Food: Bramble, ivy and wild herbs
Lifespan: Up to 16 years

Muntjac Deer are also called 'barking deer' as they bark loudly if they are alarmed.

The smallest British deer, the Muntjac, has a reddish-brown coat. The male has small antlers and tusks. All Muntjac deer are descended from deer that escaped from Woburn Park in Bedfordshire in the early twentieth century. They live on their own or in pairs, in sheltered areas that provide protection from the weather and from predators.

Feral Goat

Size: 50–60 cm
Latin name: *Capra hircus*
Habitat: Woodland and farmland
Food: Grass, leaves, bark and heather
Lifespan: Up to 15 years

Large horns

Dark coat

Feral goats can be found in remote and mountainous areas such as parts of North Wales and the Scottish Highlands. Their coats can be grey, black or brown. Both males and females have horns.

Short-beaked Common Dolphin

Size: 1.7–2.6 metres
Latin name: *Delphinus delphis*
Habitat: Sea
Food: Fish and squid
Lifespan: 25–30 years

A large group of dolphins is called a 'pod'.

As its name suggests, this is one of the most common dolphins in the world. The Common Dolphin's fins and tail are dark grey to brown. Their underside is off-white in an hourglass shape. They swim fast and can often be seen leaping out of the water. They are very noisy, too, and make a range of different sounds.

Bottle-shaped beak

Bottlenose Dolphin

Size: 2.8–4 metres
Latin name: *Tursiops truncatus*
Habitat: Sea
Food: Fish, crustaceans and squid
Lifespan: Up to 40 years

Blowhole

Bottlenose Dolphins have a pointed, short beak and a steep forehead which has given them the name 'bottlenose'. They are dark grey. They have a blowhole on top of their head through which they get air, although they can stay underwater for several minutes. They are very sociable and live in groups of between 5 and 15 dolphins. They like to follow boats and are often seen leaping out of the water beside them.

Harbour Porpoise

Size: 1.4–1.9 metres
Latin name: *Phocoena phocoena*
Habitat: Sea
Food: Fish, squid and crustaceans
Lifespan: Up to 12 years

Pectoral fin
(also known
as a flipper)

Harbour porpoises live in the shallow waters
of coasts and estuaries. There are estimated to be
350,000 living in the North Sea. They have a rounded nose
and a dark grey tail and fins. Their sides are slightly speckled.
They are sociable animals and sometimes hunt for fish in groups.

Minke Whale

Size: 8–10 metres
Latin name: *Balaenoptera acutorostrata*
Habitat: Sea
Food: Small fish
Lifespan: 30–50 years

Minke Whales can swim at a maximum speed of 40 km per hour.

The Minke (pronounced 'minkee')
Whale is found in seas off the west
coast of Scotland and around Ireland. They are
slim in shape and have a pointed head. Often seen
in shallow waters, they are best viewed from out at sea.
On their flippers, they have a white band that is noticeable
in clear water. Sometimes, they travel in groups of two or three,
but they are usually seen on their own.

Common Seal

Size: 1.8–2 metres
Latin name: *Phoca vitulina*
Habitat: Sea
Food: Fish
Lifespan: 20–35 years

Rounded face

The smaller of Britain's two seal species,
the Common Seal has a rounded, disc-like face.
They are brown or grey with dark spots and v-shaped
nostrils. Females are much smaller than males, although females
live for 30–35 years, compared to 20–25 for males. They are mostly
found along the east coast of Britain from Norfolk to Orkney and Shetland.
They are very agile in the water and can reach speeds of up to 30 kph. While
diving for fish, they can stay underwater for ten minutes, however they are
often seen out of the water soaking up any sunshine.

Grey Seal

Size: 2.5–3 metres
Latin name: *Halichoerus grypus*
Habitat: Sea
Food: Fish
Lifespan: 20–35 years

Grey Seal pups have a white coat when they are born. They get their adult coat after about three weeks.

Speckled fur

The Grey Seal is the largest of the two British seals, more common off the west coast of Britain. Half of the world's population of Grey Seals are found around our coastline. Grey Seals have longer, more pointed heads than Common Seals and are blue-grey. They are often seen with just their head and neck clear of water. Strong rear flippers push them through the water and their powerful upper body is used to haul themselves out of the sea onto steep rocks.

How to look for mammals

As mammals can be shy creatures, you could search for signs that the animals have been around. Look on the ground and near the bottom of trees for hollows of burrows and dens. Trees may have scratch marks, and nuts and seeds may have teeth marks. There may be traces of fur on or near gates and fences. See if you can find any track marks by burrows or in mud or sand.

Track marks

Keep a record of any tracks that you find. Copy them into your notebook and write down the date and the place you discovered them. Notice which are front feet and back feet. These track marks are life-size.

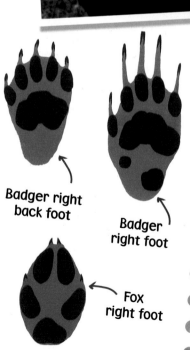

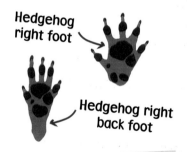

Hedgehog right foot

Hedgehog right back foot

Badger right back foot

Badger right foot

Fox right foot

Droppings

Look out for droppings, too. These are often used to mark a mammal's territory. Make a note of the size and colour of the droppings, but do not touch them.

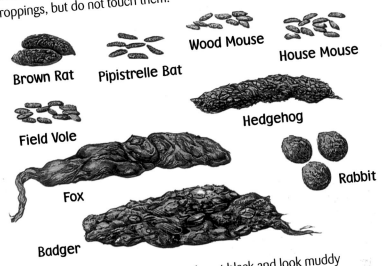

Brown Rat

Pipistrelle Bat

Wood Mouse

House Mouse

Field Vole

Hedgehog

Fox

Rabbit

Badger

Hedgehog droppings are usually almost black and look muddy because of the many earthworms that they eat. They are 1.5–5cm in length, cylindrical and about 1cm wide.

Mouse droppings are found along trails frequently used by mice. They are small, black and rod-shaped, with pointed ends.

Bat droppings are dark-brown or black in colour and cylindrical in shape. They may be found beneath the entrance to a roost, on window sills, stuck to walls or on the ground.

Badgers leave their droppings in shallow pits close to the sett.

Fox droppings are very black and often contain lots of hair or feathers. They are usually left in visible places, such as on a stone, log or high ground.

Look around you. Can you track down a mammal?

How to attract mammals to your garden

There are many ways to encourage mammals to your garden. You could grow plants that have a strong scent at night, such as evening primrose. The scent will attract insects that bats eat. Sunset is a good time to watch out for bats.

Make a food table

You could build a food table for voles and mice in a bush or small tree. Put a piece of flat wood in the middle of some branches and these mammals can use the branches as pathways. Cover the table with chicken wire to protect it from larger mammals. Put food on the table just before dusk. Raisins, seeds, unsalted nuts and fruit are good. Look for teeth marks and animal droppings the next day.

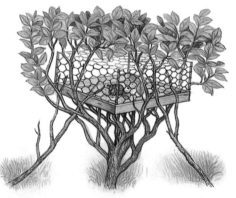

Make a hedgehog shelter

In winter, hedgehogs need a safe place to hibernate. Build a box shape with wood that hasn't been treated with chemicals (that a hedgehog might breathe in while it is sleeping). Cover the house with a sheet of thick polythene to protect it from rain. Put a plastic pipe leading up to the entrance so that the hedgehog can get in and out. Cover with leaves. Do not disturb them while they are hibernating.

Put out food in winter for those mammals that don't hibernate.

Further information

Useful websites

www.mammal.org.uk
Information and downloadable factsheets on all British mammals as well as information on species that might become extinct.

www.wildlifetrusts.org/wildlife/species-explorer/animal/mammals
The Wildlife Trusts are the largest group of UK voluntary organisations dedicated to protecting wildlife and wild places everywhere. Their species explorer page gives you photographs and descriptions of British animals, fish, amphibians and birds. You can also find a nature reserve near you.

www.wildaboutbritain.co.uk/british/mammals
Provides short descriptions about each mammal as well as information on all British nature, from birds to amphibians as well as trees and wild flowers.

www.ptes.org
The People's Trust for endangered species. Read about Britain's endangered species and find out why some mammals need help.

www.thefoxwebsite.org/faq/index.html
Answers to all your questions about foxes.

www.bats.org.uk/pages/bat_habitats.html
Information and photographs of all our British bat species.

www.scottishwildcats.co.uk/wildcat.html
Find out more about Scottish Wildcats.

www.marine-conservation.org.uk/ukseals.html
Find out more about Britain's seals.

www.bds.org.uk/deer_species_overview.html
Find out more about Britain's deer.

Useful books

100 Things You Should Know About Nocturnal Animals by Camilla de la Bedoyere (Miles Kelly, 2009)

Animal Neighbours: Badger, Bat, Hedgehog, Fox, Hare, Mole, Mouse, Otter, Rat by Michael Leach and Stephen Savage (Wayland, 2010)

British Wildlife Detectives' Handbook by Camilla de la Bedoyere (Miles Kelly, 2008)

British Wildlife Handbook (edited by Belinda Gallagher) (Miles Kelly, 2013)

RSPB First Book of Mammals by Anita Ganeri and David Chandler (A&C Black, 2011)

Wildlife Watchers: Small Mammals by Terry Jennings (QED, 2010)

Usborne Spotter's Guide: Animals, Tracks and Signs by Alfred Leutscher (Usborne, 2009)

Investigate what mammals are living in your local area!

Glossary

antlers bones that grow from the head of deer

arched curved

beak the nose or 'snout'. Also known as a 'rostrum'

blowhole the hole on the top of the head of a whale, dolphin or porpoise through which they get air

burrow a hole in the ground made by an animal for shelter

coarse having a rough surface

conservationist someone who is trying to look after and preserve nature

crevice a narrow opening in a rock or wall

dawn the time of the morning when it is first getting light

den the resting place of an animal

descended to be related by blood

droppings animal waste

dusk the time of day just before night

endangered species list a list of all species that are in danger of becoming extinct

extinct a species that no longer exists

fur farm a place where animals are kept for their fur

flippers the two fins on each side of a dolphin, porpoise or whale (also known as pectoral fins)

groom to brush, comb or lick to keep clean

habitat the place where a plant or animal lives in the wild

herbivore a mammal that eats vegetation

herd a group of mammals that live together

hibernate to spend winter sleeping

hind back or behind; or a female Red Deer

introduced to bring to a country for the first time

mate to come together to produce offspring

native belonging to a place or country

nocturnal awake at night

pectoral fin one of two fins found on each side of a whale, dolphin or porpoise. Also known as a flipper

predator an animal that hunts and kills other animals for food

prey an animal that is hunted and killed by another animal for food

roost a place where birds or bats rest

saliva the colourless liquid that is produced in the mouth

scrape a dip in the ground in which an animal rests out of sight

shed to lose or take off

species a group of animals or plants that are similar

tamed to take a wild animal and make it obedient

territory an area that an animal, or group of animals, claim as their own. They mark the territory with scent

tusk a long pointed tooth that sticks out from the mouth

vegetation plants, trees and bushes

venomous poisonous

Index